Macrophant 3D

W9-CMU-128

A Phantom 3D® book by Barry Rothstein & Jim McManus

Acknowledgments

Most of these shots were taken clueless to the identities of our subject plants and animals. Fortunately several friends and acquaintences stepped forward and challenged themselves to find them. They are: Lynn Troy Maniscalco, Terry Wilson, Karen Rusiniak, Jerome Rainey, James Comstock, Laura Wheeler, Elaine Tubinis, Dorothy Von Zumwalt, Eric Marx, Betsy Rothstein, Joy Demain, Maureen Adler at the El Dorado Park Nature Center, Kathy Musial at the Huntington Botanical Garden, Shelly Mitchell at Paleaku Gardens Peace Sanctuary, and Sharona Belcher at Hui No'eau Visual Arts Center. We also found quick and useful information on the phone app "Plant Net." We liberally used wikipedia and basic search data to enhance the descriptions.

From the 3-D photography community we'd like to thank David Kuntz, who proofed text, provided the concise definition of "stereo pair" on the previous page, and made the cool "3D" text graphic on the cover and top of this page. James Comstock also consulted on the cover selection. Thanks to George Themelis (aka "Dr. T", www.drt3d.com) for his inspiring 3-D images, and for the manipulations he made on the Lumix 3-D lenses I use. Without his advances, this book would not exist. Thanks to a guiding light, Masuji Suto, whose StereoPhoto Maker PC software and 3dSteroid phone and tablet app have improved the lives and work of thousands of stereographers around the world. Thanks to John Jerit and American Paper Optics for their 3-D glasses and long time support. Thanks to Brian Cohen for printing consultations, and to Wendy McManus for her support and help on image selection.

I feel fortunate to have convinced Jim McManus to join me on this project. I wanted to make the best book I possibly could, and realized that I could not do so alone. Jim's skills and passion made him the obvious choice.

First edition, first printing: November 2020. Printed in the USA. 3-D glasses made in the USA.
Published by 3dDigitalPhoto.com, Copyright 2020 by 3dDigitalPhoto.Com, all rights reserved. No part of this book may be reproduced in any form without written permission from 3dDigitalPhoto.com
Phantom3D® is a registered trademark of Barry Rothstein
ISBN-10: 0-9769494-3-1   ISBN-13: 978-0-9769494-3-5

Dedicated to Ray 3D Zone, the daddy of us all

To best enjoy this book ... (continued from the previous page)

capture and replicate it for others to see. Viewing a phantogram is best when your eyes are at the same angle to the printed page as the camera was to the rectangle, so we recommend you lay the book flat on a table and move your head (or slide the book) forward or backward until it looks just right. Because phantograms imitate normal vision, real objects can often merge seamlessly into the photographs. Add a rock or a twig or flower or leaf onto the anaglyph image and see what happens. Move your head left and right, up or down, and watch the effect on the images. Phantograms are incredibly interactive.

In most cases I didn't know much about the plants I was shooting, but recently did learn more about them. The identities of the images and some shooting notes are on the back pages of this book, and for those we couldn't determine, check out http://macrophant.com, which I'll update as more information comes in. I'd welcome and appreciate your input. If you know about one I didn't identify or if I got any wrong, please email me at barry@3ddigitalphoto.com.

I'm a lucky man. I walk my dog Pepper every day subconsciously hunting beautiful, intricate moments of reality and nature. Phantograms are unique, and superior at showing these shapes as they live in nature. In an imperfect way I replicate what I see, ... from a point of view and through a specific window. I invite you to share my addiction, and if you do make some yourself, please share them with me.

Finally, if there seems to be vastly more flora than fauna images, I agree, and apologize. I love good macros of bugs and other small animals. Unfortunately the nature of my hovering two handed approach tends to repel animals from hanging out in my shots.

Barry Rothstein

For over 25 years I've enjoyed opening people's eyes to the "Third Dimension" by using a variety of homemade twin-camera 'stereo' 3D rigs, enabling me to capture scenes of life all around. Upon viewing, the images spring to life in a way that only 3D can achieve. Ever since building my first stereo camera, remembering how much I enjoyed View-Master reels as a kid, I've been combining 'old' principles of photography with 'new' digital technology to create 3D photographs that reveal details not possible to perceive with an ordinary 2D picture, offering an enhanced sense of reality and heightened emotional impact when seeing stereo photographs or videos.

One of my favorite ways to share 3D with everyone has always been the "anaglyph" format, where glasses with red & cyan colored lenses are used to achieve the 3D effect by separating two images (one meant for each eye) from a single one. I find that these anaglyph versions have many advantages: they can easily be viewed by anyone with normal vision using inexpensive glasses, they can be viewed at any size and from any distance, and they can be printed at least twice as large as any side-by-side 3D format in the same amount of page space, allowing for a lot more detail to be enjoyed. Over the years I've worked to develop a method of producing anaglyphs in all their full-color glory, a feat which is difficult due to the existence of heavy color filtration (removal) in the standard red/cyan 3D glasses. For example, a blue object would appear bright in the right eye (blue lens) and dark in the left (red); this mismatch (or 'rivalry') causes visual confusion and discomfort for the viewer.

The usual solution is to just throw out all the color, and create a black & white anaglyph instead, robbing the scene of much of its potential realism... I think that black & white is sometimes a great artistic choice, but our life is in color!

Recently I needed to produce a fairly large amount of anaglyphs to submit for image approvals during a 3D project for Niagara Falls; our goal was to produce stereo side-by-side images (on film slides) for a permanent exhibit in the new Cave of the Winds visitor pavilion, but I was able to really refine my anaglyph creation process. Now I'm bringing all of my cumulative experience on the subject to this book, which represents a 'first' in terms of printed anaglyph quality... you are witnessing the debut of the "McManaglyph" process, retaining the image's proper color hue & saturation when making into an anaglyph, while also eliminating the common problem of retinal rivalry.

Thank you to my friend Barry Rothstein for getting me involved in this amazing project... I've always been a fan of his photos & techniques, and I'm honored to help him in this recent endeavor to bring beautiful 3D images to the world.

Drop by my website - www.lifeis3d.com - for stereo discoveries, galleries and information, as well as custom items & services, or to contact me about 3D

Jim McManus

Steps in Producing a Phantogram

Illustration 1: when the subject is entirely within the reference frame

Many to most people will only look at the pictures in this book, but in case you're curious about how this is done and/or want to do some yourself, I thought to provide a couple of two-page spreads to explain the process.

Producing a phantogram is by far easiest when the subject is entirely within the reference frame, with at least a little wiggle room to spare. For an example of how to work an image in which the subject extends onto or beyond the reference frame, flip to the next page.

A phantogram can be produced in any old version of Adobe Photoshop 7 and beyond, and any CS or recent version. It can also be accomplished in open source GIMP software, or in Stereo-Photo Maker. The key software requirement is being able to perform a "perspective crop," in which an image can be cropped to four independently defined corners. For clarity sake in this example I used Photoshop.

The left eye image and the right eye images are worked independently, one and then the other. Which you do first or last is unimportant. Choose the cropping tool (⊭) and roughly select the cropping area by dragging from one inside corner of the reference frame to the opposite corner. Once the area is selected, a box near the top opens with some options, including a check box with the word "Perspective." This box must be checked. Once checked it will remain that way, so you should only need to do this once.

You'll now want to zoom in some number of times by hitting the <CTRL> and the plus (+) keys, I'd recommend to 200%. Using the scroll bars to navigate, grab the corners of the selected area and carefully position them to the inside corners of your reference frame. The order you do them doesn't matter. Once all four are done hit <ENTER>.

Once the perspective crops are done, the next step is to re-size them to the original proportions of the reference frame. I use a nested set of wooden frames, all with the same aspect ratio as a standard sheet of paper, so I re-sized both left-eye and right-eye images to 8.5" x 11" at 300 dpi.

That's pretty much it. In order to make an anaglyph image you'll combine the red channel of the left eye image with the green and blue channels of the right eye image.

StereoPhoto Maker will easily do it for you, and it includes some nice anaglyph options that are helpful to deal with difficult colors such as when there's a lot of red in the image.

In Photoshop there are a few ways to make an anaglyph image from a stereo pair, and for the sake of simplicity I refer you to a phantogram tutorial at:

http://3ddigitalphoto.com/phantograms.pdf

Original left eye image

Original right eye image

Original left with perspective crop selected

Original right with perspective crop selected

Left eye image after cropping and resizing to actual proportions

Right eye image after cropping and resizing to actual proportions

Steps in Producing a Phantogram

Illustration 2: when the subject overlaps the reference frame

Unless you're strong in Photoshop skills, this page's descriptions will probably seem pretty obtuse, so I invite you skip them and move on. For those who continue I didn't intend this page to be an adequate start-to-finish guide for do-it-yourselfers. Mostly I'm trying to show anyone interested how I do what I do.

When the subject overlaps onto your reference frame, you have three basic choices: 1) forget about the image and move on; 2) plod ahead and create a problematic image; or 3) get creative and improvise. This involves extending the image area beyond the edges of the reference frame and masking out and erasing some of the image. Masking in this way has the added benefit of creating a dramatic thru-the-window effect which works very well in some images. Even when the subject does fall entirely within the reference frame, this approach can be used for for that effect.

In this example the subject barely overlapped onto the reference frame, and only on the right side, but even so, it was my best shot of this plant, so I opted to work it. When doing my perspective crops, I extended the window to the right edges of the frames. This left me without a true corner to crop to, but that's a simple work-around, I adjusted the crop so the crop line ran perfectly through the right upper corner I could not use. Similarly my finger got in the way of the bottom left corner, which happens often, but no problem, when lining up the crop I had the bottom and left frame sides as guides to position that crop corner.

After the perspective crop and re-sizing the two images, I added guidelines (shown as light blue) to define the masking area. The guidelines must be identically placed in both the left and right images. From there I did a Select All, then used the Rectangular Marquee tool to de-select the interior rectangles. Effectively I was defining an area to erase around the periphery of the images, still leaving the main subject of the images in place.

Next I zoomed in and using the Magnetic Lasso tool, de-selected the sections of the subject that went beyond the masking guidelines. In this image the edges of the subject were sharply defined, making that task easy. When they're less sharp and blend into the background I often work between the Magnetic and Polygonal Lasso tools to accomplish the masking.

Once the masking area was defined, I erased the selected area. Next I used the guidelines to crop the left and right eye images. If done correctly and the guidelines were placed exactly the same for both left and right eye images, the resulting images after this crop will be exactly the same size.

An unfortunate problem with my masking approach and printing this book on a 4-color CMYK press is that it creates a fair amount of ghosting. Ghosting happens when one eye gets information intended for the other eye. A perfect example is the large anaglyph image on the adjoining page. At its upper right through your right eye there appears to be a shadow. Without 3-D glasses on the "shadow" looks to be a muddy light blue. It was originally cyan, part of the image intended for the left eye. CMYK doesn't have a good equivalent of RGB cyan, a critical color for anaglyph viewing, so ghosting occurs..

Original left eye image with perspective crop area selected

Original right eye image with perspective crop area selected

Left eye image after perspective crop and resizing. Masking guidlines added.

Right eye image after perspective crop and resizing. Masking guidlines added.

Masking selected

Masking selected

Left eye image mask erased and cropped

Right eye image mask erased and cropped

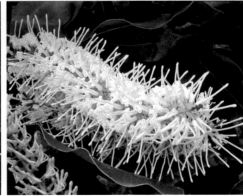

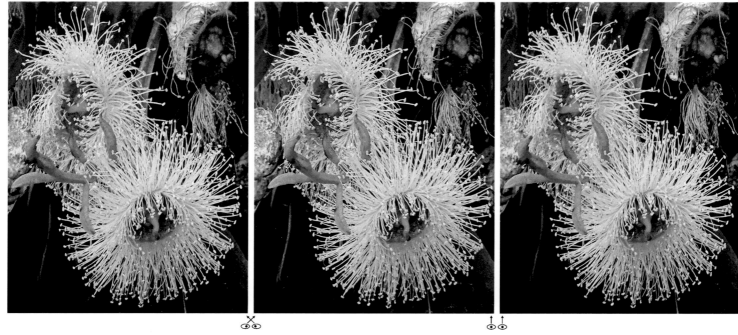

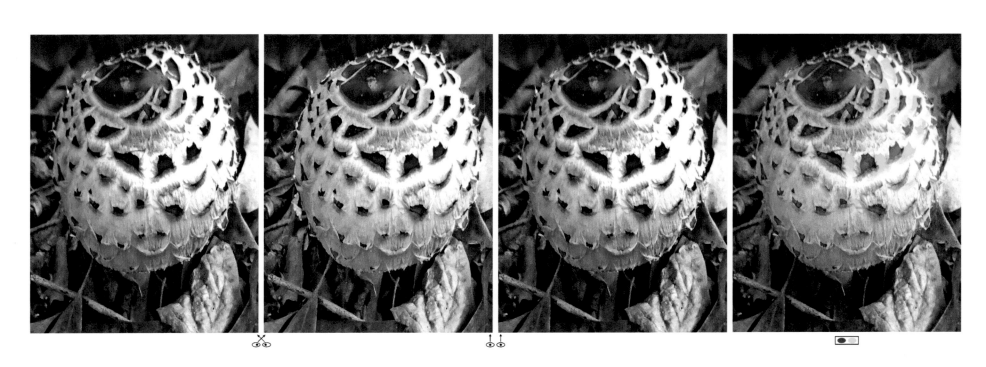

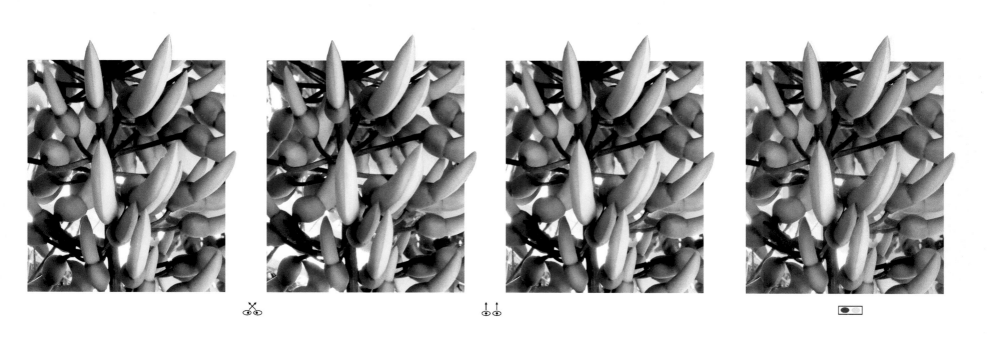

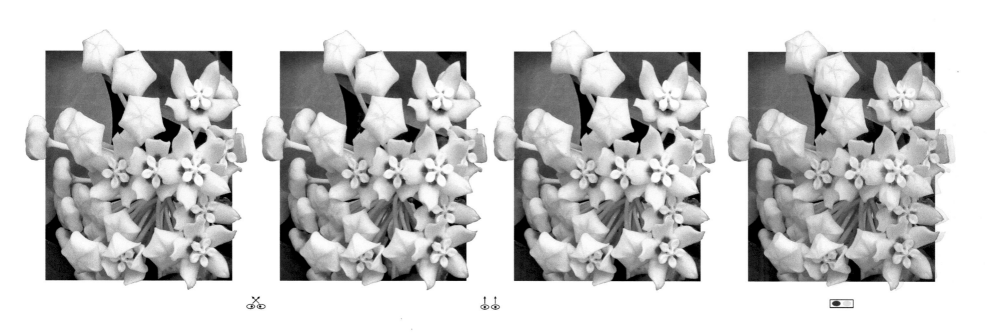

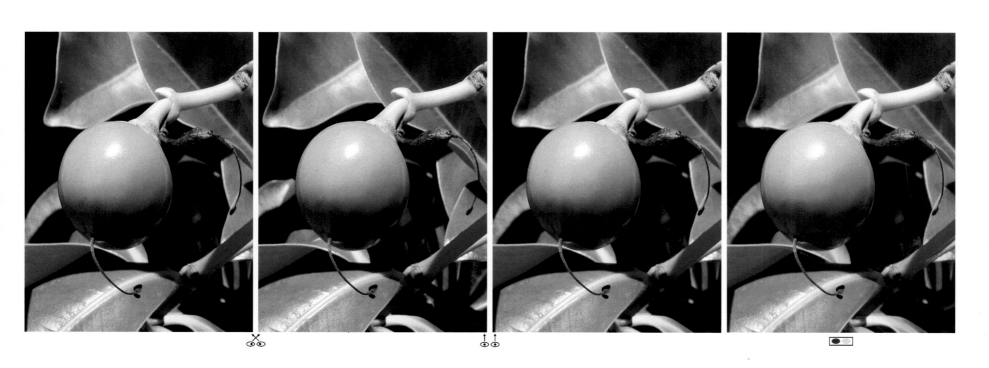

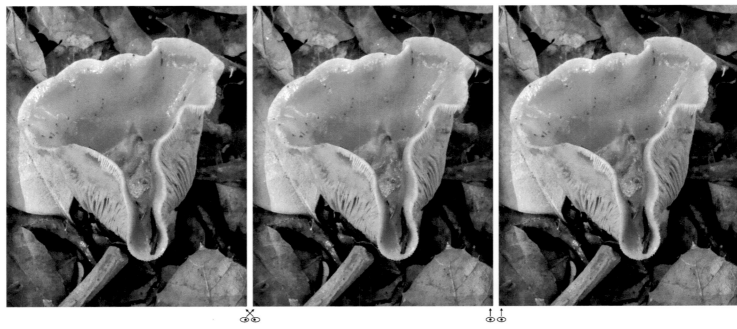

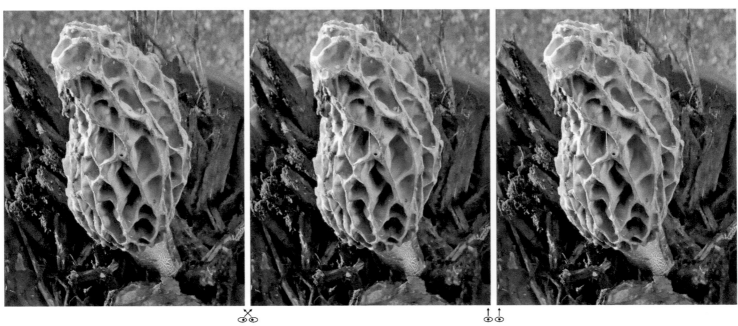

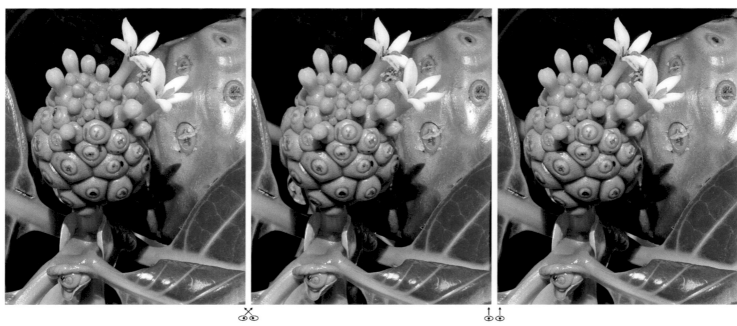

Image Identification and Notes (in order of appearance)

Cholla cactus bud. Edible if properly prepared, said to taste like a combination of green bean, artichoke heart and asparagus.

Working title: Desert Outpost
Shot in Long Beach, California

Grevillea banksii var. fosterii White-Form. White flowers occur on long dense spikes.

Working title: Swirley
Shot in Long Beach, California

Euphorbia resinifera aka resin spurge is native to Morocco on the slopes of the Atlas Mountains.

Working title: Quartet
Shot in Las Vegas, Nevada

Euphorbia also know as "spurge"

Working title: Euphorbia
Shot in Long Beach, California

Magnolia grandiflora, this is a magnolia seed. Native to the southeastern United States.

Working title: Magnolia Seed
Shot in Long Beach, California

Unsure of what type of cactus this is. If you know please email me.

Working title: Coronet
Shot in Las Vegas, Nevada

Passiflora incarnata aka passion flower, a fast-growing perennial vine with climbing or trailing stems. Passion fruit is sweet and seedy.

Working title: Passion flower & fruit
Shot in Long Beach, California

Cirsium aka thistle is a flowering plant characterised by leaves with sharp prickles on its margins.

Working title: Deep in
Shot in Cathlamet, Washington

Isomeris arborea aka Bladderpod is native to the Santa Monica Mountains and the Mojave desert. Harlequin beetle.

Working title: Harlequin Feast
Shot in Long Beach, California

Macadamia integrifolia aka macadamia nut. This is its blossom. Native to rainforests in south east Queensland and northern New South Wales, Australia.

Working title: Macadamia nut blossom
Shot in Kona, Hawaii

Echinops bannaticus aka Blue Glow or blue globe thistle is in the sunflower family, native to southeastern Europe.

Working title: Spikeball
Shot in northwestern USA

Phlomis fruticosa aka Jerusalem sage is native to Albania, Cyprus, Greece, Italy, Turkey and countries of the former Yugoslavia.

Working title: Topdown
Shot in Long Beach, California

Pulsatilla vulgaris aka pasqueflower. In the buttercup family, native to calcareous grassland in Europe. This was a roadside weed.

Working title: Country Charm
Shot in northwestern USA

Either a Western Shaggy Parasol Chlorophyllum brunneum or Shaggy Mane Coprinus comatus.

Working title: Fungal globe
Shot in Long Beach, California

Trichocereus pachanoi aka San Pedro cactus is a fast-growing columnar cactus native to the Andes Mountains.

Working title: Curvaceous
Shot in Long Beach, California

Tragopogon porrifolius aka Salsify is cultivated for its ornamental flower and edible root. This one was growing wild near a river.

Working title: Spiral
Shot in Taos, New Mexico

Agapanthus aka Lily of the Nile or African lily. Native to South Africa.

Working title: Joi de Vie
Shot in Eutin, Germany

Euphorbia ammak aka Candelabra Spurge is native to Saudi Arabia and Yemen.

Working title: Sunbleached
Shot in Long Beach, California

Either Arctium tomentosum aka woolly burdock, or Echinops exaltatus aka Russian globe thistle. Another roadside weed.

Working title: Fuzzballs
Shot in northwest USA

Unsure what type of mushroom this is.

Working title: Catching the light
Shot in Long Beach, California

Phacelia aka scorpionweed or heliotrope is native to North and South America.

Working title: Purple monster
Shot in Long Beach, California

Taraxacum aka dandelion.

Working title: Galaxy
Shot in Long Beach, California

Pennisetum alopecuroides aka Fountain grass is an ornamental grass native to Asia and Australia.

Working title: Achoo
Shot in Long Beach, California

Yucca gloriosa aka Spanish Dagger is a flowering plant native to the southeastern United States. This is its blossom.

Working title: Luscious
Shot in Long Beach, California

Eucalyptus globulus aka Tasmanian blue gum is a species of tall, evergreen tree endemic to southeastern Australia. This is its blossom.

Working title: Eucalyptus blossom
Shot in Seal Beach, California

Eryngium planum 'Blue Hobbit' aka Sea Holly is a compact perennial with spiny, egg-shaped, purplish-blue flower heads.

Working title: Pinwheel
Shot in northwest USA

Aeonium arboreum aka green tree aeonium, tree houseleek, or Irish rose, is a flowering subtropical succulent subshrub.

Working title: Yellow swirl
Shot in Long Beach, California

Callistemon salignus aka willow bottlebrush is a in the myrtle family Myrtaceae, and is endemic to eastern Australia.

Working title: Bottlebrush
Shot in Long Beach, California

Tricholobivia hybrid combines large flowers with brilliant colors. It blooms during the day several times a year.

Working title: Fuschia blossoms
Shot near Boulder City, Nevada

Rosa banksiae aka Lady Banks' rose, a flowering plant native to central and western China. It is a vine rose that grows over other bushes and trees.

Working title: Paradise Road
Shot in Topanga, California